Abortion, the Bible, and the Christian

Donald P. Shoemaker

Baker Book House
Grand Rapids, Michigan

First Printing, July 1976
Second Printing, March 1977

Copyright © 1976 by
Hayes Publishing Co., Inc.
All Rights Reserved

ISBN: 0-8010-8109-2

Baker Book House edition published
by special arrangement with
Hayes Publishing Co., Inc.

CONTENTS

FOREWORD

It is 1963. Carolyn L., three months pregnant, hesitantly steps into a small dimly-lit room. Through the dim light she sees a "doctor" wearing plastic gloves. He is standing next to a square table on which are several surgical tools which *appear* to be clean.

"Take off your clothes, I haven't got all day," he says sharply, but there is no place to put them. She drops them on the floor.

"Is this what I paid two hundred dollars for?" she asks herself silently. Still, it seems her only alternative, for she cannot seem to endure the thought of letting this unwanted pregnancy ruin her young life. She decides to take her chances.

But now it is a decade later and a Supreme Court decision has radically altered the whole scene. Susan B., in spite of greatly-widened access to birth control information, has found herself unexpectedly pregnant. A trip to a dimly-lit "clinic"? Not at all! Susan, through the help of a local abortion referral service, has been informed that an abortion is readily available if she decides she wants it. Inconvenience will be minimal, cost reasonable (she may even qualify for state assistance), and she is assured that she will have the "best" of medical care in a nearby clinic. The guilt and trauma that might have accompanied her into the darkened "clinic" of a decade ago are supposedly a thing of the past, for society's attitudes, said the referral service, have progressed to where no girl wanting release from an unwelcomed pregnancy need feel any remorse.

Much has changed, hasn't it? And yet multitudes, including many women who have experienced abortions, are unconvinced that today's permissive attitudes toward abortion really serve the best interests of women, society, and especially unborn life. For example, Dr. Bernard N. Nathanson, M.D., once a militant crusader for abortion on demand and former director of New York's first and busiest abortion clinic now regards abortion as the taking of human life and feels that a legal climate completely permissive on the issue threatens the fabric of society (*Good Housekeeping*, March, 1976).

I well remember the first time I heard the phrase "abortion reform." I was a graduate student in Indiana at the time and as a concerned Christian and American I generally aligned myself with political views considered "progressive." If something needs reform, let's reform it! I confess too that I did not know what the term *abortion* meant! When I came to understand this "abortion reform" trend, I saw it as an issue being placed unjustly beside the great movements toward human dignity and personhood in our history and in our lifetime.

It is my hope that this discussion on abortion will inform you on the issues at stake and the direction you might take. I do not want you to be uninformed as I once was. I also hope you will see that a "live and let live" position cannot be acceptable either.

Such thinking will erode our moral fabric and soothe us into irresponsibility. Advocates of abortion will frequently charge that the anti-abortionist is trying to impose his values on society whereas the pro-abortionist is protecting free choice. This is not true! For all the talk of freedom and self-determination, the abortion movement is at its heart a movement denying rights to a silent segment of humanity and soliciting public sanction, support and subsidy for its own cause. Silence against this can be destructive.

As we begin this study together let me give two clarifications which will explain the limits of this work. First, this study is intended to be introductory. I am more interested in laying a foundation than in putting every stone in place. You will find at the end some recommendations on additional material for those who wish to dig deeper. I have tried to be informed on this issue and fair in handling the material. If I am brief with some of the points I make, you must trust that the reason is to be in keeping with my purpose, not because I have studied the issue only superficially.

Second, this study is evangelical in outlook. I am writing as a Christian who has accepted the control of Christ over his life and the ethics of Holy Scripture over his decisions. I am not here to prove Christianity, but to base an ethical position upon it. If you disagree with my premise, please grant me the liberty to hold it, and evaluate my thoughts as to their loyalty to my commitment. I hope that you will not reject either my premise or my ethical decision without first investigating them.

In all fairness, you owe the same depth of inquiry into the Bible and other literature which establishes my position as I have given to the pro-abortion side.

To introduce you to this subject, I will first discuss the legal and ethical developments involving unborn life which have created today's issue and climate. Second, I will give reasons why Christians should be concerned about abortion trends. Third, I will consider how the Bible must be our authority and what teachings it presents. Finally, I will suggest a course of action a Christian might consider.

Donald P. Shoemaker

1

WHAT IS THE ISSUE WE FACE?

The present-day abortion issue centers around the changes in American thinking reflected in legislation which started in 1967 and which culminated in the U.S. Supreme Court decision of January 22, 1973.

Colorado became the first state to permit legal abortion (for very restrictive reasons). By 1971, a total of seventeen states and the District of Columbia had followed either by a change in law or by judicial order, New York being the first to have legal abortion-on-demand. Whereas in 1966 there were only 8,000 legal abortions in this country, 400,-000 were estimated to have taken place in 1971, and over one million in 1975. In California, almost 342,000 abortions were performed during the first five years of its permissive law, increasing annually to 138,584 (reported) in 1972.

A study released in February, 1975, by the most influential pro-abortion group in the nation, the Planned Parenthood Federation, noted that almost 900,000 legal abortions were reported in 1974. It found that the Supreme Court's decision on abortion had two major effects in the years 1973 and 1974. First, the number of legal abortions increased significantly, and, second, legal abortions began to be distributed more evenly throughout the nation.

This study predicts that the number of legal abortions will continue to increase for some time to come. Since almost no states require reporting of abortions and since there still are many illegal abortions, the total number is unknown but may be as much as double the reported numbers.

Newer laws were enacted to allow more latitude than older laws (which generally limited abortions to cases in which the life of the mother was at stake). These newer laws were presumably designed to provide certain safeguards and checkpoints with the intent of stifling the illegal abortion business without at the same time licensing abortion-on-demand. In practice, however, the sections of the laws which permitted abortion for reasons of "mental health" were given the broadest possible interpretation, allowing in effect abortion-on-demand. Of course, abortion-on-demand is the ultimate goal of the pro-abortion movement, both in practice and in legislation.

The United States Supreme Court decision of January 22, 1973, climaxed the six-year fight by pro-abortionists against restrictive abortion laws. This court decision ruled that during the first three months of pregnancy the woman's right to an abortion is largely absolute. From then until "viability" the woman's health becomes a matter of greater concern, and during this time the court allowed the states a certain say in where, how, and by whom the procedure can be performed. From viability until birth, the court took note of "potential human life" and felt that the state now has *two* interests. During this stage of pregnancy, the state may even "proscribe" abortion except when a licensed physician states that an abortion is needed to protect the mother's "life or *health*." "Health" was then defined to include almost any type of social distress as judged by the mother. This has, in effect, removed all protection by law from the lives of children at any time prior to birth. Its practical effect has been to allow generally unrestricted access to abortion to any who want it in the first six months of pregnancy (few doctors will perform abortions after six months).

Put simply by one pro-abortionist, before 1967 the law said, "No!" From 1967 to 1973, it said, "Yes, you may have abortion-on-demand as long as you call it something else." Since the court decision of 1973, the law says, "You may have abortion-on-demand and feel free to call it what it is!"

Stating it again, the abortion issue reveals itself this way: either (1) the unborn is not a human life, and therefore no moral issues are at stake and abortion should be an elective procedure available for those who want it; or (2) the unborn is (at least for a time) a "potential human life" and thus certain safeguards against abortion may be in order; or (3) the unborn is a human life or "person" in the full legal sense of the word and is thereby entitled to all the protection afforded any other human life. Furthermore, since the unborn child is unable to defend himself, he deserves the special consideration of the strong for the weak. As such, he may not be killed by abortion except in the gravest of circumstances.

You will find my personal conviction siding with this third statement, for I acknowledge the person-hood of the unborn at every stage of the prenatal period. Throughout this booklet when I speak of "abortion" I am speaking of the willful killing of an unborn human life in all cases other than to save the life of the mother. In other words, I am dealing with this issue as it has developed in the 1960s and 1970s. For those extremely rare cases when, rather than being able to save both lives, a doctor and family must reach a decision, I leave the matter in the hands of principled people. We are speaking here of a different situation.

2

WHY WE SHOULD BE CONCERNED

The abortion movement is trying to overlook the moral dimension.

Abortion advocates tell us that an abortion is a medical matter and thus involves only a woman and her doctor. The doctor's presence is only to insure the woman's physical well-being, not to moralize on the procedure. Legislators should keep out of the whole matter, for the issue is medical and not moral. Counseling should be solely to inform a woman with a problem pregnancy of her option and to be supportive of her, whatever her decision.

Now, this thinking assumes some rather weighty presuppositions which deserve to be tested. Legislation is the process whereby men set limits and establish policy according to certain assumed values. Through legislation we declare that men are limited by more than just what they *can* do. Let's call this limitation set on us by our individual human abilities the horizontal dimension. Legislation says that man is also faced by a moral "ought" and "ought not" which determine what he *should* and *should not* do. Let's term this the vertical dimension.

An example of these two dimensions at work can be found in the area of human rights. The Fourteenth Amendment to our Constitution declares that all citizens deserve the equal protection of the law. Legislation such as this prevents a man from arbitrarily denying basic human rights to another individual. It has been the basis for the many efforts in our day to bring the full rights of citizenship to every American. In short, this amendment limits what one *can* do by what he *ought not* to do.

The Bible requires us always to temper what we *can* do in terms of what the revealed will of God says we *ought* and *ought not* to do. Jesus, when tempted by Satan to turn stones into bread (well within His power—the horizontal dimension), replied that His power could not be used indiscriminately, that is, without taking into account the Word of God—the vertical dimension (Matthew 4:4).

One who advocates abortion as solely a medical issue assumes that neither man nor God has any just ground for imposing a moral "ought." We do not believe that this assumption is correct. It is found wanting when put beside Scripture, medical findings on the unique nature of unborn life, and the basic respect for humanness which has given us our Western values to date.

The very real issue of organ transplants today is causing some doctors to ask for legislative action giving clear definition to the point of time when life ceases, so that removal of an organ for transplanting can be done without fear of reprisal. What are they saying? They are recognizing that issues involving the definition of life and death are not simply medical matters. There must be an "ought" and an "ought not" limiting what medicine can do by what it should do. Some vertical lines are needed.

How contrary, then, to say that vertical lines should not exist at the other end of life's spectrum. Abortion is a medical procedure involving a tiny living, growing, and even moving, sleeping, and crying human being. We must tell man what he may or may not do to this living human regardless of other factors involved. We must draw vertical lines here, too.

After two serious accidents on the street in front of a school near my home, it became apparent that the street lines needed to be repainted for added safety. It had become clear that the children's safety was imperiled by having the center line too close to our side of the street. Even though this was technically an issue for skilled surveyors and painters to decide, would anyone argue that this was only a technical matter and that no moral issues were involved? Of course not, for the children's safety and lives were at stake, and this introduced a moral dimension making corrections urgent! Only foolishly would one argue that this correction was simply a technical issue and without any moral concerns. In the same vein, we must argue that abortion transcends the medical field and must also involve moral and theological values.

The abortion trend represents a change in many basic values.

As a Christian I am alarmed by the extent to which recent trends related to permissive abortion are affecting our value system. Whereas Scripture places a premium on the joys of the home, the worth of child-bearing and love for kin, we see these coming out second-best to the pursuit of career, the overplayed population explosion (at least in America), and a materialism which can seemingly afford almost everything except another child. The Bible gives warning that in the last days "natural affection" (normal affection between parents and offspring) will wane. I wonder if we are seeing a prime example of this today.

Counseling procedures and an absolutized "right to privacy" have eroded the parent-child relationship which is overwhelmingly affirmed by Scripture. When a thirteen-year-old is allowed to have an abortion apart from the consent and knowledge of her parents, we have every right to question whether or not the correct relationships and the highest values are being preserved.

The shibboleth "every child has a right to be wanted" is given as grounds for abortion without attempting to change basic attitudes which cause us not to want children. Overlooked is the tragedy of the dramatic drop in adoptable (and badly wanted!) infants due largely to the abortion trend. Overlooked also is the proven fact that unwanted pregnancies do not produce unwanted children any oftener than wanted pregnancies.

The abortion movement has not kept its own house in order.

Little research is necessary to uncover the frequent cases of kickbacks, incompetent surgery, lucrative referral services, wealthy clinics, and bags of aborted babies found outside incinerators. To this must be added the illegal abortion business which is much with us yet.

On December 19, 1970, the *Los Angeles Times* reported the survival of a baby girl after an abortion in New York City on August 28, 1970. The girl, according to the article, "appeared to be beyond the 24-week period for the operation prescribed by law." This is only one case of a failure to make certain that abortion procedures are operating within the intent of the law. I recall the comments of a staff psychologist at one California hospital whose job it was to determine whether an expectant mother's psychological condition warranted an abortion under the grounds of "mental stress." This psychologist's response was that there was never any doubt in her mind whether or not she would approve the abortion—only how the approval would be justified in words. This was clearly outside the spirit of the California abortion law.

Pro-abortion "counseling" procedures which claim to give "all the facts" to an inquirer so that she can make a responsible decision usually ignore entirely the facts known about the development of the baby in the womb as well as the real danger of permanent physical damage to the mother, and rarely give any post-abortion counseling. Every woman is at least entitled to this. Is it asking too much to suggest that someone considering an abortion be shown an accurate pictorial sequence of developing fetal life? Is it honest to depict an abortion as the removal of "fetal tissue" rather than as a process which begins with a living independent human being and ends with a dead one? Is it fair to quote (highly questionable) statistics referring to a low death rate from abortions when in reality one life is lost with every abortion? I am simply asking for *all* available facts to be given, so that a responsible decision can truly be attempted. I cannot grant those who omit or distort these facts the right to label themselves loving and progressive!

To accept abortion, our concept of "human worth" must be changed.

What gives man his value? The fact that he "is"? Or the fact that beyond being "there" he meets certain definitions imposed by others? This is extremely basic and important.

One who believes that personhood means simply "human existence" as a living being will stress the scientific findings on the humanness of the unborn. At conception the genetic code determining humanness is there. The basic organs—heart, brain, kidneys, etc.—develop remarkably early. Brain waves are discernible as early as the sixth week (and the presence or absence of brain waves is being suggested as the proper determinant of life or death). When one says that a four-week-old embryo does not look human, we must ask him to peer deeper than simply at what is visible to the unaided eye, for science tells us of amazing complexities of human existence possessed by the unborn, including the unique human make-up of forty-six chromosomes.

At three weeks, before the mother may even know she is pregnant, her developing baby already has impressive internal development. Only one-tenth of an inch long, he or she possesses the beginnings of eyes, spinal cord, nervous system, thyroid gland, lungs, stomach, liver, kidneys, intestines and heart. The primitive heart, which begins its halting beats as early as the eighteenth day following conception, is now beating regularly, sending a blood supply totally independent from the mother's through the embryo's own tiny system. By forty-five days, about the time of the mother's second missed period, the baby's skeleton is complete in cartilage, the buds of milk teeth are appearing, and the unborn child can make the first movements of his limbs and body, although it will be another twelve weeks before the mother notices movements. Sixty days after conception he can grasp an object placed in his palm or make a fist, and his heartbeat can be listened to with a commercially available instrument in the doctor's office. These remarkable facts about fetal development are known because of our more refined techniques and equipment for studying preborn human life. As this science becomes even more sophisticated, we will learn still more about the complexities of preborn life.

Scripture, too, alerts us to the fact that man is made in God's image (Genesis 1:26). Man has worth because of who he is, not because of what he might become. Scripture warns us not to rise up against another human being to do harm, kill, or slander because of his worth. Ancient Israel was to treat the "stranger in the land" with respect, not to demean him because he is not "like us." Reminded of the fact that they too as a nation had been enslaved in Egypt and robbed of personhood and worth, they were not to mistreat their fellow man. Jesus warns that treating a person as less than human falls into the same category as murder itself. The helpless and poor deserve extra care, not highhandedness and abuse. Scripture thus affirms a person's worth, dignity, and right of personhood because he is an individual member of the human race. Nothing need be added to you to make you valuable. You have worth because you *are*.

When we move from this understanding of personhood to one which places an emphasis on function, value, or relationship to the rest of society, we begin to see man's worth differently. Man now is seen in terms of usefulness and utility. As situation ethicist Joseph Fletcher says in defending abortion, "The fetus is not a personal being since it lacks freedom, self-determination, rationality, ability to choose either means or ends, and knowledge of its circumstances."

By such definition (quite questionable even in some of its details), we exclude the living human fetus from humanity at least in degree, and also endanger all other categories of human life which fail whatever test we set up. The new order of

Hitler's Third Reich first had to redefine and dehumanize the status of those they wished to subjugate or destroy, and then they could translate this philosophy into action.

It is not my intent to discuss "mercy-killing" or care for the hopelessly ill, though a discussion such as this leads us in that direction. It is quite relevant to note that euthanasia may some day be performed for the same reasons that abortion is: physical defect, mental defect, being unwanted, being a burden. The twisted ethic that allows one can be used to allow the other.

The important difference between abortion and euthanasia is that abortion *almost always* involves the death of a healthy human being who, given normal and sensible care, could have a full future ahead of him or her.

3

DECIDING THIS ISSUE AS A CHRISTIAN

No individual or society operates without a moral framework. Even the law-breaker must function within a moral system for the label to have meaning. The question to be decided here is: By what authority do we build our moral framework in which we decide the abortion issue? Will we presume some humanistic system as true for our decisions, or will we decide from a Christian theistic framework? Let's consider some of the options and see how they relate to the abortion issue.

First, some insist that each individual should be his own authority (manipulated morality). Let each man determine his own morals, and allow the same right for the other person. A sincere conviction that his system meets his own needs is all that is necessary. Morals are what I make them to be.

One medical voice justifies abortion on this basis. "They have a disease which is the problem pregnancy, for whatever reason, so as a doctor you cure the disease to make the patient well. Thinking of it in those terms, it is easy to deal with and solve." The point seems to be, "If I change the terminology and convince myself, I eliminate the problem."

Scripture warns of the danger to a society which comes when "every man does what is right in his own eyes." The theme of the Book of Judges is moral anarchy such as this and the heartache which results. The very existence of society requires us to reject the idea that every person has a right to be his own god!

Second, some suggest that majority opinion should be the determinant when setting moral values (majority morality). Simplified, this means, "Let's vote, and the decision of the largest body becomes our morality." Morals are not fixed, but are flexible, and fluctuate with the changing thinking of evolving society.

In evaluating this approach to morals, it must not be ignored that this position justifies the morals of the majority *no matter what they are*. The ancient right of the father to determine whether his offspring would live and the wholesale execution of six million Jewish people during World War II are thereby justfied because society consented! Even a democratic system such as our recognizes that majority morality must be checked by the rights of the minority and other values, and so we have the constitutional process to prevent abuse of the principle of majority rule. This means we recognize that there must at times be an authority outside of and above the consensus of society as a determinative on morals. And the same is true in the abortion controversy, for society must also have some values other than majority opinion when dealing with unborn life.

Has "majority morality" influenced the thinking on abortion? *Newsweek* (July 19, 1971) quotes one medical opinion: "Abortion is finding its place as a perfectly acceptable and valid health measure. We no longer think of it as a crime." If this is correct and if this trend continues, we will begin to see discrimination building against those who are personally opposed to abortion. Dissenting doctors will find limitations placed on their ability to practice gynecology, since society will not offer positions to the dissenter. Nurses have already found their jobs imperiled and doctors have been subject to lawsuits. In a recent court case, the testimony of a noted obstetrician was characterized as unreliable because of his staunch anti-abortion stand.

Abortion advocate Lawrence Lader applies "majority morality" to the question of whether guilt should be expected after one has an abortion. "In highly civilized cultures, abortion without guilt has become the social norm. Society can make the experience a traumatic one, or a psychologically logical one." As Christians, however, we must recognize a difference between *subjective* guilt which may come and go with society's attitudes toward our decision and *objective* guilt before the standards of a living God.

A third possible basis for authority is to have our moral decisions made by an elite, and handed down from the top (mandated morality). One is amazed by the growing thinking toward increased governmental decision-making and control over population size and quality. When the population does not regulate itself the state offers to do the regulating through taxation, birth-control, and easy-access abortion. Our big questions at this point are: "Who is going to sit at the top and make the decisions?" and "Are these decisions being guided by the ethics of Scripture, or will other expedients be the guide?" Should total regulation of the right to life be put into the hands of the few, our ultimate prayer will be that we can sit on the committee!

How should Christian thinking evaluate these three approaches to morality? I would suggest that, while not casting aside any of these approaches totally, we should study them selectively—retaining what is right and profitable and rejecting what is wrong and harmful in light of the Biblical system of morality.

The Christian starts his thinking with a belief that there is a living God whose Word is Holy Scripture (revealed morality). Because God exists there also exist certain values consistent with who God is. If God created the world, made mankind in His image and placed him in the world, and then gave man standards to live by which reflect the character of God, then these realities are to serve as the basis for our morals. If God gives each human life worth and declares that human life must not be indiscriminately destroyed, and if from Scripture we can find that unborn human life is recognized as having this same worth, then we must call the world to subject itself to this truth. If God designed man and his existence, man will experience meaningfulness and self-affirmation to the extent that he appropriates the will of the Designer.

Consistent with Christian theistic morality as described above, I believe that abortion must be defined as *the destruction of a human life in violation of the Sixth Commandment—"You shall not commit murder."* We will now strive to show that this correctly expresses Scripture and the general tenor of Christianity.

4

THE BIBLE AND THE PRO-ABORTION ARGUMENT

During the permissive abortion trend several reasons have been submitted for justifying an abortion. Beyond all of these is the ultimate argument that no reason should be necessary because abortion is a woman's basic right.

First, it is suggested that abortion should be allowed if, in the opinion of the mother, a birth would work economic hardship or difficulties in the family's or individual's social pattern (the socioeconomic argument). To let the argument stand is to leave unanswered a more basic issue: "Are the life-values and priorities which seemingly necessitate the abortion correct from a Biblical perspective, and more valuable than the loss of life?"

Even above socio-economic values, Scripture considers blessed the individual graced with childbearing. *"Behold, children are a gift of the Lord; The fruit of the womb is a reward"* (Psalm 127:3).* Godly women are assured by the apostle Paul that through bearing of children self-fulfillment is found (I Timothy 2:15). Financial and family planning along with a conscientiousness toward one's social role all play an important part in life, but decisions in each area

---

*Scriptural quotations are from the *New American Standard Bible,* copyright 1971, The Lockman Foundation, La Habra, California.

must have beneath them a Biblical system of priorities.

A second suggestion is that abortion is justified when there is the likely prospect that a child will be born mentally or physically defective (eugenic argument). Again, it is right to raise the question of priorities and life-values, but we must also ask, "Is there a Biblically-established right to die?" This would be difficult to assert. The Book of Job clearly leaves this prerogative of life and death in the hands of God. *"Though he slay me, yet will I trust in him"* (Job 13:15). Let us allow for a moment, however, that to die is a person's right. The last thing I would want is for another person to exercise this right in my behalf! Let this be *my* decision, if you please! Or is the eugenic abortion argument really saying that abortion in such cases is justified because this new human might be a burden to *others* and those others want him killed so they will not be burdened?

The Scriptures assure us that the Christian life is a time when God takes steps to bring the believer to strength and maturity. Often this involves situations in life which are not in themselves pleasant. The writer of the Epistle to the Hebrews says, *"For whom the Lord loves he disciplines, and he scourges every son whom he receives"* (12:6). If I wrongly rid myself of a situation which God intended to be a part of my life experience, I am now requiring Him to exert new and harder pressure upon me. In the midst of personal and family suffering the Old Testament man of faith, Job, could testify, *"The*

Lord gave and the Lord has taken away; blessed be the name of the Lord." The writer then states, *"In all this, Job did not sin, nor did he blame God"* (Job 1:21, 22).

Third, medical reasons are suggested as grounds for abortion. Such cases are actually and increasingly quite rare, and what one decides in regard to them will not bear on the basic problem of permissive laws. Of the first 254 abortions reported in California after passage of its permissive law, only 15 were for medical reasons, whereas 214 were for "psychiatric" reasons. As Dr. Christopher Reilly says, "There are some clear-cut, non-psychiatric medical reasons for induced abortion, but they are becoming quite rare."

The basic issue here is not unlike those already mentioned. Does the mother's physical health warrant the killing of her tiny son or daughter except in cases where it is evident either one or both will die without an abortion? A motto from Proverbs might be instructional at this point: *"The spirit of a man can endure his sickness, but a broken spirit who can bear?"* (Proverbs 18:14). My physical condition is important, but more so are the qualities I build into my spirit to sustain me. Never should we violate the divine ethic in pursuit of physical comfort or convenience. In effect, we do not turn the stones into bread when God's will does not permit it.

The apostle Paul teaches us concerning an infirmity which he suffered, terming it his *"thorn in the flesh."* We have no clear idea what it was

29

(which is fortunate, for we can therefore apply his lesson to many situations), but we do know that he earnestly wished to be free of it (II Corinthians 12:7, 8). Paul learned that instead of removing it, God used him *through* his infirmity to a greater degree than he could imagine!

A fourth ground suggested for abortion is pregnancy resulting from rape or incest. Admittedly, we find this a very difficult point of discussion. Yet, if human life possesses the value that Scripture teaches it does, it seems wrong to justify abortion in such cases. Our society has largely determined that the guilty rapist may not be executed for his crime. Are we then to mete out capital punishment upon the innocent unborn?

God forbid that we should regard any situation as so tragic that God could not have prevented it if He so chose. As Christians we have received the precious promise that no testings will overtake us except those God has permitted men to experience. God is faithful (I can put my trust in Him and know He makes no mistakes). He will not allow us to be tested above what we can stand, but will with the testing make a way of escape that we might be able to bear it (see I Corinthians 10:13). If God has allowed a burden to be placed upon me, and if in the light of His Word there is no legitimate means whereby the burden can be removed, He promises to sustain me as I bear it. The proof of God's ability to empathize with our difficulties is found in the life of Christ. Our Lord while on earth experienced and conquered testings in every aspect of human stress, and invites us to approach Him to find *"grace to help in time of need"* (Hebrews 4:15, 16).

God's intent, it seems to me, is to give sustaining grace in such situations. Should God's Word allow alternatives other than I have presented, I am more than ready to abide by them. We do well to realize, too, that relaxing our principle of the overriding value of a life at this point will make it both easier and more logical to justify abortion for other cases of mental trauma. In reality, justifying abortion for rape or incest is not a separate category, but simply an extension of the argument that mental anguish justifies killing another human life. Rather than solving mental stress through killing, proper resolution of the stress calls for supportive counseling which builds acceptance of self and of circumstances as they are.

Fifth, abortion is suggested as allowable as long as the unborn life is not yet viable. Here the argument turns from the probable cause or result to the nature of the preborn human. The point stressed is that as long as the fetus has not reached a point of development where it can survive outside the womb, he or she can be killed (aborted) without concern as to moral values. But viability is a very fluid criterion. By it the unborn says, "I do not directly need my mother any longer." Before viability, the unborn requires the controlled environment and nourishment that the womb supplies. It is interesting that, while abortionists are trying to push legalized abortion as close to birth as possible

(*Time* reports "abortions" of babies so developed that they cried for hours before dying), medical science is pushing viability closer and closer to conception. Indeed, when science finally succeeds in fertilizing an ovum with a sperm artificially and then is able to nourish the embryo apart from the mother through the whole gestation period (test tube baby), there will be no such thing as a viability factor!

The ultimate goal of the pro-abortion movement is that abortion should be an absolute right and that no law should interfere except to safeguard the health of the mother during the procedure. No reason should have to be given for the abortion. Some have made this issue, unfortunately, the vanguard of women's liberation. Many years ago, feminist advocate Margaret Sanger said, "No woman can call herself free until she can choose consciously whether she will or will not be a mother." Groups such as Feminists for Life, however, have worked to show that abortion and women's rights are not necessarily wed to each other.

From a Christian standpoint the absolute right to an abortion based on the argument that every woman has a right to control her own body meets three objections.

First, only God has absolute rights. The only rights I have are really privileges God allows me to possess out of grace. He may remove them at any time. Mankind has no absolute rights.

Second, no one has rights to his own body. Whatever liberties God has extended to us, the freedom to do with our bodies as we wish is not among them. The Christian is instructed, *"Or do you not know that your body is a temple of the Holy Spirit who is in you, whom you have from God, and that you are not your own? For you have been bought with a price, therefore glorify God in your body"* (I Corinthians 6:19, 20). Even the non-Christian is constrained by his responsibility to God as creator. Paul likens God's relationship to him as a potter working with clay (Romans 9:20, 21). In marriage, especially, one's control over his or her own body is delegated to the marriage partner. *"The wife does not have authority over her own body, but the husband does; and likewise also the husband does not have authority over his own body, but the wife does"* (I Corinthians 7:4).

Third, even if the mother had rights over her own body, the developing preborn baby is not part of her body. This is simple biological fact. The preborn child has a separate blood supply, separate circulatory system, separate heartbeat, separate brainwaves, and very early its own separate will! The mother's body would "reject" the fetus's body and abort it naturally were the placenta unable to counteract this natural tendency. If the skin of the preborn baby were transplanted to the mother, her body would reject it. In its splendid portrayal of prenatal life, *Life* magazine (April 30, 1965) notes that from the day of fertilization the human embryo is antigenetically foreign tissue to his mother.

These, then, are the basic arguments undergirding the current permissive abortion movement.

Many who would defend staunchly the right of postnatal human life to live will yet use these arguments to defend killing prenatal human life. However, the continuity of human existence is so strong from fertilization through every stage of gestation and after birth until death that the burden of proof is certainly on the pro-abortionist to justify a difference in attitude toward the preborn baby as opposed to the postborn baby. Ethicist Paul Ramsey has observed,

> Until we are given a moral argument for abortion in certain sorts of cases that would not also be an argument for infanticide in the same sorts of cases, then the [argument] proposed [for] abortion is now morally the same as that for infanticide, even granting there is no tendency toward the production of the latter institution. Abortion would be (unless and until we are clearly shown otherwise) morally the same sort of "slaughter of the innocent." Those who believe this is the case have every right to say so. No good reason can be advanced why the use of pungent language should be reserved for those who plead the cause of distressed, conscious lives needing the relief for which abortion is proposed.*

*Paul Ramsey, "Reference Points in Deciding About Abortion," *The Morality of Abortion*, p. 86.

5

THE BIBLE AND THE
ANTI-ABORTION ARGUMENT

The findings of physiology and genetics clearly point to the designation of the unborn as a human being. Though each of us began life as only one cell, this one cell had all the information and power needed to multiply and specialize toward the goal of forming a complete human body. One who denies the humanness of the fertilized cell must bear the burden of proof. If not human, what kind of life is this as determined from genetic evaluation?

The Christian, however, does not formulate his ethic on these findings primarily, but relies on the witness of God's revelation for ultimate authority. What grounds do we have from Scripture to support the definition of abortion that has been suggested?

In the Old Testament, we find a strong tendency to deal with the unborn as a definite personality and to protect his life from harm. God is presented as intensely and intimately involved in the welfare of the fetus. It was Jewish belief that no child was conceived without the work of the Spirit of God. They felt that there were three partners in the production of any human being—the Holy One, and the father and mother. We wish to consider several Old Testament passages before turning to the New Testament.

Job 10:8-12

*"Thy hands fashioned and made me altogether,
And wouldst Thou destroy me?
Remember now, that Thou hast made me as clay;
And wouldst Thou turn me into dust again?*

*Didst Thou not pour me out like milk,
And curdle me like cheese;
Clothe me with skin and flesh,
And knit me together with bones and sinews?*

*Thou hast granted me life and loving kindness;
And Thy care has preserved my spirit."*

Job is speaking here about the process of his formation. In poetic language his development passes before our eyes as he compares his formation to the pouring out of milk into a container, suggesting fertilization. Then God begins to "stir the milk," to turn it into cheese, the finished product. This portrait of fetal development shows God's direct involvement and interest from start to finish. According to verse 12, God takes our frame and develops it marvelously. The unborn is granted life and favor and possesses a personal spirit.

Isaiah 49:1, 5

*"The Lord called Me from the womb;
From the body of My mother He named Me."*

"And now says the Lord, who formed Me from the womb to be His servant. . . ."

Jeremiah 1:5

"Before I formed you in the womb I knew you,
And before you were born I consecrated you;
I have appointed you a prophet to the nations."

These two passages (the first being a prophecy concerning Christ) point to God's ministry of grace and His purpose in behalf of the unborn. Just as God is actively at work in the process of physical formation, so He is earnestly at work preparing certain individuals for spiritual ministries.

It is true that the phrase "from the womb" can be a reference to God's involvement while the individual is yet in the womb, or it can mean God's involvement from birth onward, in which case it would be translated "out of the womb." The key is that this phrase is connected with formation, and thus refers to the period within the womb, not the period beginning with birth. Jeremiah 1:5 emphatically bears this out, for it declares that God "knew" Jeremiah before birth and he was already set aside and designated a prophet.

In all these verses, personality is ascribed to the unborn. He is called to salvation, set aside for service, and made a recipient of grace—unlikely blessings for mere "tissue"!

Psalm 139:13-16

"For Thou didst form my inward parts;
Thou didst weave me in my mother's womb.
I will give thanks to Thee, for I am fearfully
and wonderfully made;
Wonderful are Thy works,

And my soul knows it very well.
My frame was not hidden from Thee,
When I was made in secret,
And skillfully wrought in the depths of the earth.
Thine eyes have seen my unformed substance;
And in Thy book they were all written,
The days that were ordained for me,
When as yet there was not one of them."

This fascinating psalm contains Scripture's most complete account of prenatal development. Its basic theme is the inescapable presence of God. Should we try to flee to heaven, the grave, darkness, or even to the depths of the sea (vv. 7-12), God is not escaped. Our only proper response to His all-pervasive presence is to be open before Him, letting Him search and purge our hearts (vv. 23, 24).

Why is God so intimately concerned about man? The answer is found by looking at man's prenatal development. When David begins verse 13 with the word "For," he is about to tell us that God's constant interest in man is simply the natural interest that a maker would have in a very special product! These verses which speak of unborn existence are not without difficulties in translation, but we are able to glean their important lessons nonetheless.

Why is God so interested in man? He formed man's inward parts (literally, "kidneys"—a reference to man's most deep-seated organs, possibly speaking also of his most secret and tender emotions). He "weaved" man in the mother's womb—a graphic reference to the process whereby the basic frame of man is covered and laced by series after series of sinews, muscles, blood vessels, and tissues. God seeks us now because He made us then, and from our earliest moments we were in His tender care!

As the psalmist considers the wonder of this truth he exclaims (I paraphrase), "I will give thanks to Thee, for in regard to these marvelous facts [God's active interest in the unborn] I am wonderfully made [I stand apart as something special— different from all lower forms of life]." Edward J. Young gives to us the impact of this verse:

> How awe-inspiring is the birth of a child! In the mother's womb the strange act of conception has taken place. Life has come into existence. A growth occurs. And this embryo will come forth one day from the body of the mother and a human being will be born. Truly these are fearful things. To think upon them is to begin to realize, at least to an extent, the greatness of the God who can create and bring life into existence. And we should think upon these things! The very wonder of the circumstances under which life is conceived and the embryo formed should produce fear within our hearts, for we are then in the presence of the Author of Life.*

In the fifteenth verse the psalmist exclaims that, though the work of forming the embryo was not observable to man, God was no stranger to it. God Himself was hard at work skillfully forming the complicated tissues and organs that compose the human organism. Even before there was a dis-

*Edward J. Young, *Psalm 139* (London: 1965), p. 72.

cernible form to David's human frame, God had His watchful, caring eye upon it (v. 16). The word for "unformed substance" speaks literally of something folded up into the shape of an egg and is probably a reference to the human embryo.

Though the term is difficult to translate, our versions are probably correct in describing it as something "unshapened" or "unformed." The point seems to be that although this tiny speck of living matter bore no resemblance of humanness to the eye, this does not mean that God was unaware and uninterested in it. His eye was upon it, in the active sense that He was governing and guiding its development. David's constant use of the first person in this section ("I," "me," "my") lets us know that he regarded God to be at work with him personally, not merely with some mass or tissue that later would become a person. David understands himself as a person in God's hands throughout these verses.

The marvel of this passage is enhanced by our recent ability to visualize and understand embryonic development to a degree never before possible (though even today, as the psalmist reminds us, much of God's work is secret). One has only to study the dramatic series of embryonic portraits in *Life* magazine (April 30, 1965) to appreciate the wonder of prenatal development. The Bible prods us to consider the origin of human life as God sees it and to worship Him for what He does in the womb. This passage can only evoke holy caution and respect for unborn life. God is at work, and as we observe we must worship, for the place where we stand is holy ground. Such respect for the divine origin of life is not to be found among the pro-abortionists. Theirs is an unholy intrusion into the divine laboratory to interrupt and to destroy the handiwork of the blessed Creator! God loves the unborn. This psalm will never let us forget it.

Psalm 51:5

"Behold, I was brought forth in iniquity, and in sin my mother conceived me."

The Biblical witness to the sinfulness of man traces his sinfulness not merely to what he does, but to what he is—sinful in nature. More than any other Old Testament reference, Psalm 51:5 has served to cement this concept into Christian thinking. The thought of this verse is conveyed in the words of the Westminster Larger Catechism: "Original sin is conveyed from our first parents unto their posterity by natural generation, so as all that proceed from them in that way are conceived and born in sin."

We can readily see that this verse, then, speaks to the issue of the origin of personhood as it points to the time when each person's sinful nature originates. In confessing that he and he alone is responsible for his sinful conduct the psalmist traces his sinful tendencies back to his birth and beyond that to his conception. He was "brought forth" in iniquity and even more was actually "conceived" in sin. This scarcely means that the circumstances of his conception were impure or that there is something inherently evil in procreation. David simply and clearly traces his own sinful nature as far back as his conception, and in so doing he acknowledges his own existence as going back as far as this moment of time as well.

A similar reference to personal existence from conception is found in Job 3:3, where Job at a time of personal tragedy bewails, *"Let the day perish on which I was born, And the night which said, 'A boy is conceived.' "* The verb for conception is different here (*harah* rather than *yacham*), but the concept is the same, with the important fact added that Job was a "man-child" as early as conception.

Exodus 21:22-25
"And if men struggle with each other and strike a woman with child so that she has a miscarriage, yet there is no further injury, he shall surely be fined as the woman's husband may demand of him; and he shall pay as the judges decide. But if there is any further injury, then you shall appoint as a penalty life for life, eye for eye, tooth for tooth, hand for hand, foot for foot, burn for burn, wound for wound, bruise for bruise."

Of all the Old Testament passages, none bears more strongly on the subject of abortion than this passage, for it shows how Israel was to judge a situation involving the death of the unborn.

There are some who feel this passage settles for good the question of whether the unborn is of lesser worth than the postnatal life. Does it not suggest that punishment occurs only if the unborn is lost due to a physical blow against the mother? Only the mother's life is protected by the Law of Retribution ("life for life"), according to this view. Now, I along with many others do not believe this view is the best interpretation of the passage as I will show in a moment. But even assuming it is, notice that the loss of the unborn *still* is wrong, as shown by the fine imposed. And notice, too, that even if "life for life" applies only to the mother, this does not prove that the passage regards pre-natal life as unhuman, for the same context (v. 20) dictated punishment rather than "life for life" for the man who struck and killed his slave, and we are not going to call his slave unhuman!

However, I believe a different interpretation fits this passage better. It is unfortunate that the loss of the unborn referred to in this passage is translated by our versions as the mother's "fruit" departing from her (KJV) or as a "miscarriage" (NASB). This suggests that the passage looks on the unborn as merely some kind of unshapen mass, and not as a child. The Hebrew word *yalad* is better translated in its simple sense of "child," which fits its use elsewhere in the Old Testament. Furthermore, the words "depart from her" *(yatsa)* more naturally refer to a childbirth, not to a miscarriage (note Genesis 25:25, 26, where this word "came forth" describes the births of Esau and Jacob). The Hebrew has a word to describe miscarriage *(shakol)* used in Exodus 23:26. But *yatsa* means simply "to come out," and here refers to childbirth—coming out from the womb into the world. Thus, the phrase "her fruit depart from her" in Exodus 21:22 speaks of a premature birth, not a miscarriage.

If, then, a woman is struck so as to cause her to go into labor and deliver her child, but no other harm occurs (to mother or child), a fine is imposed on the assailant. If, however, harm should come beyond this premature birth (such as loss of life to mother or child) the Law of Retribution would apply. Exodus 21:22-25 therefore affirms equal protection to the unborn, implying equal regard and worth.*

When we look at the New Testament we find the same emphasis on the personhood of the unborn and also a continuing lack of differentiation between born and unborn existence. When we add to this the blessing of the conception of Jesus the worth of the unborn is difficult to resist.

Matthew 1:18, 20
"Now the birth of Jesus Christ was as follows. When His mother Mary had been betrothed to Joseph, before they came together she was found to be with child by the Holy Spirit. . . . 'for that which has been conceived in her is of the Holy Spirit.' "

It is important to see that the divine activity is found during the time Mary was "with child"—yes, at conception itself. There is no thought here of a

---

*For a fuller discussion of this passage see Jack Cottrell, "Abortion and the Mosaic Law," *Christianity Today* (March 16, 1973), pp. 6-9.

human or (subhuman) Jesus who at birth or afterwards took a divine nature (orthodox Christianity has always regarded it as heresy to hold that the human Jesus ever lacked the divine nature). No, the divine Christ was present from conception on. The angel spoke to Mary of her unborn child as *"the holy thing begotten"* of her (Luke 1:35).

This rather detailed account of the conception of Christ is instructive to us because our human origin is not unlike His own, His sinlessness and the virginity of His mother excepted. *"Wherefore it behooved him in all things to be made like unto his brethren that He might be a merciful and faithful high priest"* (Hebrews 2:17).

Luke 1:41, 44

"And it came about that when Elizabeth heard Mary's greeting, the baby leaped in her womb; and Elizabeth was filled with the Holy Spirit. . . . 'For behold, when the sound of your greeting reached my ears, the baby leaped in my womb for joy.'"

This Gospel story is simply the report of the conversation between two pregnant women whose offspring were to play a vital role in the founding of the Christian faith. Elizabeth was carrying John the Baptist in her womb, and John was the forerunner to Jesus, who would be born to Mary. Luke 1:39-55 records the encounter. As we consider it, we gain important insights into the status of the unborn.

Elizabeth was already six months pregnant with John. Since a six-month human fetus is afforded less and less protection in our time, it is important for us to consider what this passage might say of John's status as a person. As the Virgin Mary approached Elizabeth and greeted her, her six-month-old fetus leaped for joy. More than any mere quickening, this fetal movement was a most human reaction. A six-month fetus is capable of expressing joy! John the Baptist was most probably filled with the Holy Spirit at this moment in time also, for it was prophesied that he would be filled with the Spirit while yet in the womb (Luke 1:15).

Our study of the unborn also must, at this point, consider the status of the unborn baby Jesus. We do not know how soon after the Annunciation recorded in Luke 1:26-38 this meeting between Mary and Elizabeth occurred. It was probably very soon (Luke 1:39 says, *"in these days"*). This means that Jesus was perhaps a mere zygote—not even yet implanted in His mother's womb. At least, He was very, very tiny! And we might note that it was probably the proximity of the unborn Jesus to the unborn John which produced his leap of joy, not merely the appearance of Mary the mother. When we examine it closely, our story is not just the encounter of two mothers. It is also a meeting between a fetus and a zygote! With a stroke of Luke's pen unborn children would forever have a new dignity.

Another important fact also must be seen from this passage. The term used to describe John the Baptist in these two verses ("baby") is the Greek word *brephos,* which means "an embryo; a babe;

an infant; a young child, born or unborn." From this definition and from uses of this word found elsewhere in the New Testament, we see that Biblical writers under the inspiration of the Holy Spirit felt no need to show any distinction between children before and after birth—one word sufficed to speak of both. The term as used in Scripture is broad enough to describe unborn human life (here), newborn life (I Peter 2:2 and Acts 7:19, where it describes the young lives which the king of Egypt ordered slain in an evil attempt to obtain "zero population growth" among Israel's sons—an interesting parallel, termed "subtle" and "evil" by the Bible, to the ideas of some abortion enthusiasts today) and childhood (II Timothy 3:15). We are forced by the usage of this word to affirm what we already know from biology—that childhood extends into the womb.

Beyond these two clear references to unborn life, the New Testament also gives to us an ethic and a value system that prevent us from discounting the value of human life.

In the Sermon on the Mount, Jesus taught the utter depravity of the attitude toward man that made killing a matter of definition only—a deed to be feared only if it incurred the wrath of civil authorities (Matthew 5:21). He warns that any attack upon a fellow human, any attempt to diminish him as a person or to question his worth is equal to murder in God's eyes even though technically it might not be chargeable before a civil court (Matthew 5:22). We must see that the Christian ethic must never merely acquiesce to legal definitions of murder. It must go beyond legal technicalities and assert as Jesus did that human life must not be redefined and narrowed so that attacks against humanity (individually or collectively) become justifiable because they are "within the law." The Nazi experience whereby human worth was redefined qualitatively, allowing the elimination of those deemed "lesser," must never be forgotten!

Another important ethical value is found in Jesus' discussion of the two great commandments (Matthew 22:34-40). The whole moral system which God has given is fulfilled when men love God above all else and when they love their neighbors as themselves. When men truly love their neighbors, they do not covet or kill or violate other moral laws against their fellow man. Abortion ethics at its heart is a selfish grasping at personal rights to the exclusion of others. It is a bold overpowering of the weak by the strong. Jesus said this must not be—the neighbor must be endeared by every man. And no one is more a neighbor to another than the unborn child whose heart beats in the bosom of its mother!

A comment is now in order on the Scriptural teaching concerning the human soul. I hesitate to devote much space to this, for I feel too much is made in our day of supposed "parts" of man. Scripture always deals with man as a unity, not as something we can dissect and put on an organizational chart.

But somehow some have set forth the idea that a fetus is a human body lacking a human soul, and therefore abortion is not a moral issue, for the fetus is not yet a person. Let it be said that any view like this reveals a bias toward Platonic body-soul distinctions nowhere found in Scripture.

Genesis 2:7, which must be regarded as a *locus classicus* on human personhood, declares that it is the impregnating of the life-principle (the "breath of God") into the formed clay which is man's body that constitutes man as a living being (a person). Both the forming of the body and the giving of the breath of life are works of God. Put together they form a person. We now know that both of these works are vitally a part of the gestation process from conception onward. There is no room in Genesis 2:7 for a dualism—a developing, breathing human organism which somehow lacks a "soul" in the Platonic sense. The Book of Job makes allusion to this idea when Job asserts, *"The Spirit of God has made me, And the breath of the Almighty gives me life"* (Job 33:4). Job clearly traces his origin to the moment when God gave life with His own breath—a life which commences at conception. Ecclesiastes 11:5 states, *"You do not know how a pregnant woman comes to have a baby and a living spirit in her womb."* The presence of a living, functioning human organism signals the presence of Man in all that he is. Those with Platonic bias are hard put to tell us why *birth* should be the time of the soul's implantation since birth is only a change in environment for the unborn, not a change in his or her own personal "being." Besides, Jesus spoke of a killer as one who causes death to the *body* (Matthew 10:28).*

Even in Christendom this Greek body-soul dichotomy has had its inroads with inevitable influence on the proper regard for the unborn. Aristotle had taught that the fetus is originally vegetable, then animal, finally human. Influenced by this, St. Thomas Aquinas taught that the fetus receives a soul at quickening (14-20 weeks). During the Middle Ages the fetus was regarded as human when the soul became rational—at forty days for a male and eighty days for a female! How inconsistent with both Scripture and scientific findings!

How did early Christianity, impregnated by the ethics of the Old and New Testaments, influence the world of its day as to the value of human life? Early Christianity gave to the world a renewed sense of dignity, for it saw man as created in the image of God and affirmed that God has interest in each individual both before and after birth.

A document reflecting second-century Christian thought, *The Teachings of the Twelve Apostles,* forbade the slaying of "a child by abortion," regarding

---

*For more information on the unity of man as taught in Scripture and the contrast between this idea and the Platonic body-soul concept see:

Clifford E. Bajema, *Abortion and the Meaning of Personhood* (Grand Rapids: Baker Book House, 1974), pp. 15-41.

G. C. Berkouwer, *Man, The Image of God* (Grand Rapids: Wm. B. Eerdmans, 1962), pp. 194-233.

George Eldon Ladd, *A Theology of the New Testament* (Grand Rapids: Wm. B. Eerdmans, 1974), pp. 457-59.

this as a "way of death." The *Apostolic Constitution* (an eight-volume set of ecclesiastical literature compiled in the fourth century and reflecting the views of Christian theologians in previous centuries) testifies, *"Thou shalt not slay thy child by causing abortion, nor kill that which is begotten, for everything that has been shaped and has received a soul from God, if it be slain, shall be avenged as being unjustly destroyed."*

Such teaching brought this new faith into direct conflict with the permissive attitude toward abortion in Roman society. Lawrence Lader notes, "Christian dogma came into immediate and bitter conflict with the Roman custom [that the fetus is not a human person]." He continues, "The prohibitions against abortion are essentially the product of the Christian philosophy." This is quite a statement for Christians to ponder, coming from one who is in the vanguard of the pro-abortion movement.

In summary, I submit that relevant Scriptures uphold the interest of God in behalf of the unborn, and the personhood and consequent worth of prenatal life, this also being upheld by a proper understanding of the soul. This is the position of Biblical Christianity. It supports the definition of abortion suggested earlier as the correct position for the Christian moralist and answers arguments which would justify abortion. It is most consistent with scientific findings. As today, this position brought the early church into conflict with existing counter-values.

6

WHAT CAN A CHRISTIAN DO?

Our generation and culture has cut itself from the Christian consensus which was once its ethical mooring. As a result, it is now unable to offer an ethical framework with a sufficient base to differentiate between the right and the wrong with sufficient objectivity. The Christian with his theistic morality is faced today with a golden opportunity to offer a system of living which begins with a relationship with God through Jesus Christ and provides a contrast between right and wrong that is definitive. Christianity alone can both expose wrong and change the human heart to do God's will. This route alone will ultimately satisfy both God and mankind.

For you who may now feel that I have expressed the mind of Christ on this issue and have faced it realistically, I wish to conclude with a few suggestions:

Be informed.

If you are really concerned, you should concentrate on this issue. Materials are being produced all the time by the various viewpoints on abortion. Learn to recognize non-Christian, pro-abortion errors even when they come from the lips of "respected" people. For continuing information from a nonreligious pro-life source subscribe to the *National Right to Life News*. If you have time to read only one book on the scientific side and one on the Christian viewpoint, read *Handbook on Abortion* and *Abortion and the Meaning of Personhood*. Law, medicine, and ethics are in constant motion and we must be acquainted with their directions if we are to speak intelligently of them.

Be a "progressive."

This is a much-abused term, and it needs to be rescued from those who would turn the clock back on the worth which God has given to man and woman. In many ancient societies the father had control over the right of an unwanted offspring to live. Are we to allow those who return to this ethic (with a slight shift in giving this right to the mother) to call themselves "progressive"? I think not. The truly progressive are those who know the ethics of their Christian faith and are applying them to the current moment. They are informed about the findings of medicine and moralize on these findings. They also have the mother's best interests at heart. They know from psychology that abortion is no "final solution" to mental or domestic stress, so they strive for an approach to this problem which is most loving and healthful.

Be active.

We must not sit idly by with some notion that the separation of the Christian from the world allows us to hide and ignore our responsibilities.

Proverbs 24:11, 12

"Deliver those who are being taken to death,
And those who are staggering to slaughter, O hold
them back.

If you say, 'See, we did not know this,'
Does He not consider it who weighs the hearts?
And does He not know it who keeps your soul?
And will He not render to man according to his
work?"

The Christian lawmaker must be just as ardent as his non-Christian colleague to see his morality expressed and protected by law. Sunday's religion simply cannot be divorced from Monday morning's clinic! *All* legislation is the expression of whatever ethical system is dominating the legislative halls, and the Christian's light should be shining there too.

Exiled Russian dissident Alexander Solzhenitsyn writes in an essay that the desire to transfer personal values to society at large is basic to human nature. He alerts us, however, that not all values are noble and just. Some are base, hypocritical, false and cruel. He warns, "And, clearly, whatever feelings predominate in the members of a given society at a given moment in time, they will serve to color the whole of that society and determine its moral character. And if there is nothing good there to pervade society, it will destroy itself, or be brutalized by the triumph of evil instincts . . ." (Alexander Solzhenitsyn, "Repentance and Self-Limitation in the Life of the Nation," *From Under the Rubble*,

p. 106). His perceptive words should serve as a caution against lethargy for those whom Jesus Christ commissioned to be the "salt of the earth," permeating society with His life and teachings.

As individuals, our goals can be nothing less than was the goal of the abolitionists of the nineteenth century. Their goal was to eliminate slavery (discrimination and dehumanization on the basis of skin color) in every state in the Union. Today, we must work until we have eliminated this new discrimination (against preborn humans) in every state in the Union. The goal of the abolitionists was accomplished by the Thirteenth and Fourteenth Amendments to the U.S. Constitution. Our goal can best be accomplished by a new amendment to the Constitution returning equal protection by law to all living humans regardless of age, or perfection, or place of residence (in the womb).

Until this goal is achieved, we can work diligently to pass whatever restrictive laws are possible under the Supreme Court decision, remembering that these are pitifully inadequate but may be the best that can be obtained until a federal amendment is passed (see Deuteronomy 24:1-4 in the light of Matthew 19:3-8).

We can also be active in the various "Right to Life" organizations, the pro-life activist groups found in most communities. We can write, talk, give money, parade—the list is endless.

Be considerate.

We must remember that abortion decisions do

not involve callousness at all times. Often there is much heart-searching. Frequently, women are sincerely seeking help. All too many abortionists are interested neither in them nor their offspring. Let us not be like them! Along with our pro-life convictions there must always be love and the big heart.

I attended one pro-abortion seminar and went away thoroughly disgusted by the profanity, spiritual blasphemy, dirt and grime expressed there. Let us not be like that. Pro-life people give constant witness. Make it a compassionate and loving one. However righteously indignant we may be in judging the wrong of abortion, let us always remember to hate only the sin, not the sinner.

Be firm.

Considerateness does not compromise the content of what we say. While we choose our words carefully, we must be clear to draw lines where we see them. The sin of murder is dealt with by God in the sternest terms from Genesis 4:8-12 to Revelation 21:8 and 22:15. We cannot do less.

We must not allow a professing Christian, for example, to think that an abortion unresolved before God will escape His eye. Evangelical churches must state their position most clearly so that their people will know that they take abortion as seriously as God does. This may even involve church discipline against one who willingly violated God's Word (I Corinthians 5; Galatians 6:1).

56

Be supportive.

No position against abortion is adequate without a compassionate, sensitive program to aid those with problem pregnancies. We do justice neither to the Bible nor to the person by saying, "No!" without offering support which can build a new framework of thought with which to view these problem circumstances. We would not, for example, simply call for the reinstitution of anti-abortion laws which ignore this supportive element.

We must become part of and support the telephone lifelines, the emergency pregnancy service volunteer groups, counseling programs and other measures that have grown up alongside the Right to Life groups. A congregation could, for example, develop a program to allow unwed expectant mothers to continue their schooling while also learning to adjust to their pregnancies. All programs affirming both mother and child deserve our support.

Be forgiving.

"Just as God in Christ also has forgiven you" (Ephesians 4:32).

God's Word is unbending in its standards and exacting in its penalties. But parallel to this truth is God's willingness to forgive the one who comes to Him through faith in Jesus Christ. This forgiveness stands available to anyone willing to accept it, and one who receives it should experience the same sense of forgiveness from one's fellow man.

ADDITIONAL BIBLE PASSAGES RELATING TO ABORTION

In Reference to Killing

Genesis 9:6
"Whoever sheds man's blood, By man his blood shall be shed, For in the image of God He made man."

Exodus 23:7
"Keep far from a false charge, and do not kill the innocent or the righteous, for I will not acquit the guilty."

Deuteronomy 27:24
" 'Cursed is he who strikes his neighbor in secret.' And all the people shall say, 'Amen.' "

Psalm 94:20, 21
"Can a throne of destruction be allied with Thee, One which devises mischief by decree? They band themselves together against the life of the righteous."

Proverbs 6:16, 17
"There are six things which the Lord hates, Yes, seven which are an abomination to Him, Haughty eyes, a lying tongue, And hands that shed innocent blood."

I Peter 4:15
"By no means let any of you suffer as a murderer,

or thief, or evil-doer, or a troublesome meddler."

I John 3:15
"Every one who hates his brother is a murderer; and you know that no murderer has eternal life abiding in him."

In Reference to God's Attitude Toward the Handicapped

Exodus 4:11
"And the Lord said to him, 'Who has made man's mouth? Or who makes him dumb or deaf, or seeing or blind? Is it not I, the Lord?'"

I Samuel 16:7
"But the Lord said to Samuel, 'Do not look at his appearance or at the height of his stature, because I have rejected him; for God sees not as man sees, for man looks at the outward appearance, but the Lord looks at the heart.'"

Isaiah 42:3
"A bruised reed He will not break, And a dimly burning wick He will not extinguish."

Isaiah 42:19
"Who is blind but My servant, Or so deaf as My messenger whom I send? Who is so blind as he that is at peace with Me, Or so blind as the servant of the Lord?"

Matthew 18:8
"And if your hand or your foot causes you to stumble, cut it off and throw it from you; it is better

for you to enter life crippled or lame, than having two hands or two feet, to be cast into the eternal fire."

Luke 14:13, 14
"But when you give a reception, invite the poor, the crippled, the lame, the blind, and you will be blessed, since they do not have the means to re-pay you; for you will be repaid at the resurrection of the righteous."

FOR ADDITIONAL READING

Pro-Life Materials

National Right to Life News (monthly). 5227 Lyndale Ave., So., Minneapolis, MN, 55419.

Bajema, Clifford E. *Abortion and the Meaning of Personhood*. Grand Rapids: Baker Book House, 1974.

Cottrell, Jack. "Abortion and the Mosaic Law." *Christianity Today* 17 (March 16, 1973), pp. 6-9.

Granfield, David. *The Abortion Decision*. Garden City, NY: Image Books, 1971.

Noonan, John T., ed. *The Morality of Abortion: Legal and Historical Perspectives*. Cambridge: Harvard University Press, 1970.

Scott, Graham A. D. "Abortion and the Incarnation." *Journal of the Evangelical Theological Society* 17 (Winter, 1974), pp. 29-44.

Willke, Dr. and Mrs. J. C. *Handbook on Abortion*. Revised edition. Cincinnati: Hayes Publishing Co., 1975.

Other Materials

Life (April 30, 1965). "A Graphic Pictorial Sequence of Developing Fetal Life," pp. 54-72.

Gardner, R. F. R. *Abortion, The Personal Dilemma.* Grand Rapids: Wm. B. Eerdmans, 1972.

Spitzer, Walter O., and Saylor, Carlyle L., eds. *Birth Control and the Christian.* Wheaton, IL: Tyndale House, 1969.

Stott, John R. W. "Reverence for Human Life." *Christianity Today* 17 (June 9, 1972), pp. 8-11.

The author has produced a six-page pamphlet entitled "A Pastor's Heart to Heart Talk on Abortion" summarizing the abortion issue from a Christian standpoint (available for 10¢ each or $1.00 per dozen plus postage from Donald P. Shoemaker, 2251 Knoxville Ave., Long Beach, Cal. 90815).